Ace Your Case®!
Consulting
Interviews

2nd Edition

Insider Guide

Helping you make smarter career decisions.

WetFeet Inc.

The Folger Building
101 Howard Street
Suite 300
San Francisco, CA 94105

Phone: (415) 284-7900 or 1-800-926-4JOB
Fax: (415) 284-7910
Website: www.wetfeet.com

Ace Your Case®! Consulting Interviews

ISBN: 1-58207-247-7

Table of Contents

The Recruiter's Perspective 59

Case Examples 65

For Your Reference 109

Ace Your Case at a Glance

Why Case Interviews?

- To test a candidate's analytical and communication abilities
- To see how resourceful and creative you can be
- To test how you perform under pressure

Major Categories of Case Questions

- Market Sizing
- Business Operations
- Business Strategy
- Brainteasers
- Other (International, Government)

Key Case Question Frameworks and Tools

Basics: Internal/External, Supply/Demand, Cost/Benefit, Marginal Cost Analysis, Fixed Cost/Variable Cost

Add-Ons: 3Cs, 4Ps, EVC

Luxury Class: Porter's Five Forces, Firm Analysis, Financial Analysis

Consultants' Favorite Tools: 2 x 2 Matrix, Graphs, Visual Representations of Data

The Interview Unplugged

- Consulting Case Interview

- The Bottom Line

- What to Expect

- Seven Steps to Surviving the Case Interview

- Do Firms Approach the Case Interview Differently?

Consulting Case Overview

You're pacing nervously back and forth in the career center, waiting for the interviewer to come out and call your name. You're all dressed up in your interview suit, you've got your resume in hand, you've practiced saying why you want to be a consultant a thousand times, and yet you're still nervous. Although you'd do anything short of shining your interviewer's shoes just to get a consulting job, you're deeply worried because you know that, in a matter of moments, you're going to hit that most dreaded of all interview challenges: the case question. Suddenly, you panic. Vivid memories of your last tragic interview/train wreck come flooding back. . . .

Whoa! Slow down! Take a deep breath and relax. You may not ever learn to love the case interview question, but, with a little bit of thinking—and some practice—you actually will be able to sail through this part of the interview just as easily as the resume review. WetFeet is here to tell you how.

Let's start with a simple definition. The case interview is essentially a word problem based on a real-life (or simulated) consulting situation. Thus, the interviewer might say, "Okay, Terry, suppose a client comes to you and says, 'We're thinking about going into the lightbulb business, and we want you to tell us what to do.' What should you tell her?"

Cases come in all shapes and sizes, from the simple, straightforward question designed to see how you think about a problem, to the highly complex business strategy issue that takes 20 minutes to explain and involves charts, graphs, and buzzwords up the wazoo. However, they all have one thing in common: They test a candidate's analytical abilities. They show his or her resourcefulness, how he or she thinks about problems, and ultimately, his or her aptitude for consulting.

How does the interviewer evaluate you? By watching for several things: how you analyze the problem, how you ask for additional details, how you slice through extraneous information to get to the key issues, how you pursue a particular line of thinking and stay with it, how you propose to identify the information that will allow you to solve the problem, and, most importantly, whether or not you can develop (and present) a particular framework for organizing your thoughts and answers to the case question.

Although this may seem like a daunting assignment at the start, the good news is that there are many ways to prepare yourself for this task. Armed with these strategies, and bolstered by a little practice, you ought to be able to do every bit as well as anybody who has gone before you. Surprising as it may seem, you may also come to view the case question as the part of the interview where you can really shine!

The Bottom Line

Like it or not, if you're planning to get a job in consulting, you will have to learn how to handle the case interview. Although different firms and different interviewers have different approaches to the case question, all of them use it as an important tool in selecting and screening out job candidates. Indeed, you may have to clobber ten or more cases on the way to landing a job with a major management consulting organization. Fortunately, by studying up on the case process and honing your case interview skills through practice, you'll soon be able to amaze friends and family alike with your frameworks and graph-drawing skills. Even better, when that dreaded moment in the interview arrives—and the interviewer pops the question—you'll be more than equal to it.

What to Expect

The typical management consulting interview generally consists of several parts. At a minimum, these include an introductory "get to know you" conversation, a resume review/prove-to-me-that-you're-qualified-for-a-consulting-job Q&A, a case interview question, and a follow-up "what do you want to know about us" discussion. Although the case question portion of the interview inspires the most terror, the other portions of the meeting are every bit as important. You've heard it in other contexts: don't ignore the foreplay. Insiders tell us that many candidates, even at the very best schools, have already bombed the interview long before the case question slices them into tiny little pieces. Fortunately, WetFeet is here to help. Before we dive into the rocky, shark-infested waters of the case question itself, let's spend a little time warming up. The next few sections should help you navigate the path through the minefield to the point where the fireworks begin.

Part 1: Getting to Know You

"Hey! How are you doing? What a great day for a consulting interview!" It may sound like meaningless banter (and it probably is), but the interviewer is still checking you out. First question in the recruiter's mind: Is this candidate alive? If not, the interview is likely to drag. If you are alive—and seem interested, perky, and excited about the opportunity to interview with company XYZ— then this is your chance to develop a rapport with your interviewer. Typical questions here may involve the weather, why you decided to attend Kellogg (or Stanford or Columbia or CMU or wherever), how classes are going, how the job search is progressing, what's up with the 49ers, and so on. Your key goal

here should be to show the interviewer that you have an engaging personality, are fun to be around, and would be a valuable addition to the team.

Remedial Interviewing for Would-Be Consultants

Here are a few tips from consulting insiders about points at which previous candidates have fallen off a cliff. Take note—you don't want to be the next statistic!

- Show enthusiasm for the company. How psyched will your Booz recruiter be if he suspects you're thinking, "Well, I'd really rather get an offer from McKinsey, but they already dinged me." Yeah, make that two—ding!

- Practice saying, "I reeeaally want to be a consultant—and here are the three reasons why!" Say it at night, rather than counting sheep. If you don't, the other candidates are lined up about 300 deep right behind you, and there's an excellent chance that many of them really do want a spot in the consulting leagues.

- Don't talk about yourself in a negative manner. Self-deprecation won't get you anywhere in consulting. If you don't think you can tell a 30-year veteran at Goodyear a thing or two about tires, well, maybe you should sign up for an interview when Goodyear comes to campus.

- Demonstrate that you're a fun person. How about it? Would you want to go out for beers with a cold fish (even a smart cold fish), much less spend months working together in Indianapolis?

- Be high-energy! Smile! Be excited! Sixty hours per week may not sound so bad right now, but when you've been at the client site from 8 am until 9 pm every day this week and last week, and the week before . . . Anyway, the interviewer is going to be looking for people that have the stamina and the desire to put in long, tough hours—and still come up shouting, "Please, sir. Give me another spreadsheet!"

Part 2: Prove Yourself to Me

You've had a clever little chat about the weather to demonstrate that you really are alive; you've told a good story about why you love your alma mater more than your own mother; and now it's time for the recruiter to pull out your

resume. "So, tell me about the work you did for . . ." What's going through the recruiter's mind? Something along the lines of "What has this schmoe done that shows he or she is smart enough to handle the consulting workload?" To keep sailing straight toward that case question, you'll need to demonstrate that you have had significant work experience (or a reasonable facsimile thereof), can work well with others, have the aspiration to lead, and have the intellectual horsepower to do the heavy lifting required of consultants.

How to Impress a Consulting Recruiter

Just exactly what impresses the hard-nosed consulting recruiter who has not only seen it all before, but likely has done it all before (or at least advised a client on how to do it)? Here are several tips gleaned from WetFeet's conversations with management consulting insiders. One word of caution (especially to our friends at HBS)—you'll want to walk that fine line between providing evidence of your capabilities and seeming like an overbearing braggart.

- Talk about situations in which you have assumed a significant leadership role. You might mention the challenges you faced and how you overcame them, or what you learned about yourself as a result of your experience.

- Your goal should be to demonstrate, with well-articulated examples, that you have the qualities of a Churchill, Martin Luther King, Jr., or Mother Teresa.

- Think of several examples of projects at school, at work, or in an extracurricular setting in which you were challenged and survived with flying colors. Remember, dating stories don't count!

- Prepare for the questions that you know are coming. In particular, have a good, concise explanation of why you want to be a consultant and why you specifically want to work for firm XYZ. (Hint: Don't know the real difference between McKinsey and Bain and Booz Allen and . . .? Check out the latest version of the WetFeet Insider Guide on the firm. You'll learn everything you need to know to ace your interviews!)

- Be prepared to be asked about anything on your resume. Consultants have a nose for obscure facts that can turn up pungent information. One of their favorite tricks is to take an item on the resume and turn it against you as the

basis for a case question ("So, I see you've worked in software. Do you think Apple has any sustainable competitive advantages?"). Our advice: think ahead about how each bullet point on that resume can be turned into a compelling (short) story that demonstrates your aptitude for consulting.

- Think of examples of work in which you had to use consulting-type skills. No, that doesn't necessarily mean situations in which you charged exorbitant fees for your advice. Rather, look for situations in which you had to be highly analytical or in which you had to be very resourceful about identifying hard-to-find information.

Part 3: Here Comes the Case . . .

Let's say that so far you're so well prepared that you have slam-dunked the get-to-know-you and prove-yourself-to-me portions of the interview. Admit it—you're feeling pretty good, as well you should. Now it's time for the infamous case interview. Sometimes, you'll get this question from the same interviewer who has been bouncing around all the high points of your resume. On other occasions you'll transfer to another interview room and an entirely different interviewer who will serve up "The Question." Typically, it will begin with something like, "Okay, let's say you are meeting with the CEO of a large phar-maceutical company. He says to you . . ." Now it's time for you to show just how bright and analytical you really are.

What is an example of an experience in which you took on a leadership role?

_____

_____

_____

_____

_____

_____

_____

How have you demonstrated initiative?

_____

_____

_____

_____

_____

_____

The Interview

The WetFeet Interview Coach (cont'd)

How would you define your leadership style?

_____

_____

_____

_____

_____

_____

_____

What are some key lessons you have learned about motivating people?

_____

_____

_____

_____

_____

_____

Ten Things NOT to Do in a Case Interview

1. Don't burst into tears.

2. Don't say, "I think that question really blows."

3. Don't ask if you can "plead the Fifth."

4. Don't look at notes you have scribbled on the back of your hand.

5. Don't ever say, "I don't have a clue."

6. Don't say, "Wait, what were we talking about?"

7. Don't say, "The answer is 10,000."

8. Don't say that the questions you got in your (other consulting firm's name) interview were really much more challenging.

9. Don't jump from topic to topic without explaining how it fits into a framework.

10. Don't reveal that you've been coached by the experts at WetFeet!

The WetFeet Interview Coach

Create several case questions for yourself based on your resume. (Not only will this help you prepare for possible questions, it will give you a better sense of what makes a good case question. Think about strategic or operations implications related to your previous industry or field. If you worked in a homeless shelter, for instance, a good case question might be: "Let's say your organization has had stable funding and client usage, but a new neighborhood shelter has grown dramatically. What's going on?")

_____

_____

_____

_____

_____

_____

_____

_____

_____

_____

_____

Seven Steps to Surviving the Case Interview

So how exactly does one ace the case? Although the specifics of each case question will be different, we've devised an approach that, if used correctly, will take you a long way toward giving the consulting interviewer what he or she wants. Ours is a mnemonic device for acing your case. Simply think of the words "WetFeet." Those seven letters will help your ace your case!

When the interviewer asks the question, listen carefully. Take notes if necessary. Make sure you know what the interviewer is seeking. It's particularly important to keep this objective in mind as you work your way through the dense forest of detail that may be coming your way.

Everything there? Determine whether you've been given the whole picture. If the question is unclear, it's probably unclear for a reason. Ask your interviewer for clarification. In particular, if there seems to be a gaping hole, ask about it. The interviewer may be testing whether or not you realize that there are missing pieces to the puzzle. Or he may be holding back a key piece of information to see if you ask for it.

Think before you speak. It's acceptable to spend a minute or two jotting down notes for yourself to follow, just as you would before writing out an essay for your final history exam. So take a minute and think about your answer rather than starting too quickly and digging yourself into a ditch.

Frameworks! Identify a framework, or a combination of frameworks, to help you structure your answer. Be sure to inform your interviewer how you plan to

proceed. Remember, choosing a framework isn't the goal of the exercise—it's supposed to help you structure an answer to the question. It will also help your listener (the interviewer) follow your presentation and show her how you think.

Explain your thinking methodically. Start with the most important issue first. Remember, if you run out of time part way through, you want to have already delivered your most important insights. A structure or framework will help you plan how to cover all the major points during the time allowed.

Every hint helps. Interviewers often give hints, extra data, or suggestions. Listen for them. When you hear a hint, a suggestion, or additional information, use it. Even though he may not smile and his collar may be starched as stiff as cardboard, your interviewer is likely to be a very nice person who was just as nervous as you are when he was trying to ace his case. Many interviewers will try to gently prod you in the direction they want you to explore. Listen for their clues! Use their help! They know what they are looking for and will usually try to steer you in the right direction.

Talk action. Wrap up your case by briefly summarizing how you have approached the problem and noting where you would go if you had more time. The goal of consulting is almost never just analysis. Usually, a consultant is looking for good, solid, data-driven recommendations for the client.

Do Firms Approach the Case Interview Differently?

We've heard rumors from the interview cubicle that different consulting firms prefer different types of case questions—and different types of answers. If you think you have an angle on that front, go ahead and use it, and good luck. However, after talking to dozens of company insiders at a large number of consulting firms, we've determined that the similarities in case interviewing style from consulting firm to consulting firm are far more striking than the differences. Indeed, the primary differences in style seem to come from the personalities of the individual recruiters.

Let's face it, consulting interviewers come in all shapes, sizes, and temperaments. Since consulting firms take recruiting so seriously, as a rule you are more likely to end up with a great interviewer than you are with a guy who never calls his mom on Mother's Day. On that count, well, cross your fingers and hope that you don't land a particularly obnoxious interviewer. If you do, keep your cool, do your best, and remember as you leave the confines of the interviewing cubicle that your social life is going to be a lot more exciting over the next few months than his is.

Keep in mind that interviewers usually approach undergrads differently than they do MBAs or other advanced-degree candidates. As you might expect, undergraduate case questions are usually less complex, less focused on specific business issues, and more focused on the skills that will be required of research analysts (or whatever the firm calls its undergraduate hires). In particular, the

interviewer will often push the candidate to demonstrate resourcefulness, creativity in thinking about a problem, and ability to stick with a problem and get to the bottom of it. So if you're an undergrad, don't pass out when you read through the frameworks section of this report; your interviewer won't expect you to have mastered MBA-level concepts. If you're an MBA, however, start studying and be prepared for anything!

Field Guide to Case Types

- Five Categories of Consulting Cases

- Buzzword Bingo

Five Categories of Consulting Cases

You will have an easier time successfully dissecting a case problem if you know that they come in several different forms. For the purposes of our discussion, we have grouped cases into five general types. They include:

1. **Market Sizing:** determine how big a particular problem is, or how many of x products are used

2. **Business Operations:** problems relating to running the day-to-day operations of a business

3. **Business Strategy:** questions focusing on future business strategy, usually at a top level

4. **Brainteasers:** puzzles or questions that challenge a candidate's ability to think creatively

5. **Other:** a grab bag of questions such as those drawn from a candidate's resume, macroeconomic questions, and others

The next several pages present, in greater detail, examples from each category of consulting case. We also provide tips on what the interviewer is really trying to find out. As you read through these sample questions, think carefully and creatively about how you would respond. And since our job is to help you ace your interviews, WetFeet will provide possible lines of response for a number of the classic questions in the sections that follow.

Market Sizing

What the Interviewer Wants to Know

Are you allergic to numbers?

Can you identify key drivers, make assumptions, and work out a reasonable answer?

How resourceful and clever are you?

Classic Questions

How many paint stores are there in the United States?

How many manhole covers are there in Manhattan?

What is the market for personal computers likely to be in 15 years?

Business Operations

What the Interviewer Wants to Know

Do you understand basic business issues/internal relationships?

Do you have a nose for the key issues?

Can you come up with and present a compelling solution?

Classic Questions

A trucking company operates its fleet at only 85 percent capacity. What's going on?

A bank discovers that its customer turnover is 15 percent higher than the industry average. Why?

Business Operations Variation 1: Profits Down

What the Interviewer Wants to Know

Do you understand the basic profit equations and concepts (Sales – COGS – Other = Profits; fixed/variable costs; product mix; etc.)?

Can you identify and use an appropriate framework?

Can you interpret the analysis and offer logical recommendations?

Classic Questions

A garment company has noticed a decline in profits in its women's apparel unit. What's going on?

A disk drive producer has a long-term contract to provide OEM disks at a fixed price. How can it increase profitability over the remaining term of the contract?

Business Operations Variation 2: Marketing Problems

What the Interviewer Wants to Know

Do you understand basic marketing concepts (4 Ps, channels, push vs. pull strategies)?

Can you identify and use an appropriate framework?

Classic Questions

The company has sponsored a professional tennis event for a number of years and is considering canceling its sponsorship. Should it?

A petroleum company has a new environmentally friendly gasoline. How should it price and market the product?

Business Strategy

What the Interviewer Wants to Know

Can you identify key strategic issues for a business and relate them to core competencies and mission?

How are you at industry analysis?

Can you handle the complexity of a full-blown strategy-type case?

Can you develop recommendations for action based on your analysis?

Classic Questions

A bank is thinking about going into the brokerage business. Should it?

A large, diversified petrochemical company wants to fend off a hostile acquisition bid. What should it do?

Business Strategy Variation 1: New Product Introduction

What the Interviewer Wants to Know

How do you sort through product strategy issues and market-cannibalization questions?

Classic Question

A cereal company is thinking about introducing a new natural cereal. How should it go about making its decision?

Business Strategy Variation 2: New Markets

What the Interviewer Wants to Know

How well do you understand core competencies, fit with current business portfolio, and opportunities for leverage and adding value?

What are the key tools you look at to evaluate an opportunity?

Classic Questions

Your client says it wants to begin exporting to France. Should it?

A Bell operating company is looking at opportunities in wireless data transmission. Should it invest there?

Business Strategy Variation 3: Merger or Acquisition

What the Interviewer Wants to Know

Can you identify core competencies of a company?

Can you understand dynamic forces in an industry and analyze opportunities?

Can you quantify a new opportunity?

Classic Questions

Client says it wants to buy company XYZ. Should it go ahead?

Client just purchased a venture in industry X and wants to restore the company to profitability. What should it do?

Business Strategy Variation 4: Competitive Response

What the Interviewer Wants to Know

Can you combine market data with internal resources to provide a convincing recommendation?

Classic Question

A department store chain has been losing market share to discounters. How should it respond?

Business Strategy Variation 5:
Response to Change in External Environment

What the Interviewer Wants to Know

Are you creative?

Can you demonstrate an understanding of the dynamic forces within an industry?

Can you identify and evaluate various strategic options?

Classic Questions

An automaker wants to know how a new trade agreement will affect its sourcing options.

A defense contractor that has been focusing on civilian applications asks you which to abandon as it swings back to security projects.

Brainteasers

What the Interviewer Wants to Know

Can you think "out of the box"?

How creative are you when confronted with an unusual problem?

Do you like intellectual exercises?

Classic Questions

Why are all computers putty gray?

Why are manhole covers round?

Tell me all the different ways in which you could determine whether the light inside a refrigerator is still on after the door is closed.

Other Case Types

Resume Cases; International; Government; Reengineering; Totally Random Cases

What the Interviewer Wants to Know

Did you really do what you said on your resume?

How much did you learn from your previous work experiences?

How's your macroeconomics training?

How do you handle unexpected territory and nonbusiness constraints?

Can you analyze and apply frameworks to other problems?

Classic Questions

Your resume says that you opened a distribution network in Mexico. How would you apply what you learned there to opening a similar network in Thailand?

The government of Peru wants to develop an industrial policy. What do you advise?

A nonprofit, pro bono client asks for your help in determining why its membership revenues are declining and how to respond.

Buzzword Bingo

Here are a few terms you may hear during your interview. To help you understand exactly what each term really means, WetFeet offers the following translation notes.

Barriers to entry

Translation: the case interview question, for example. (Actually, see the discussion of Porter's Five Forces for more information.)

Declining profits

Translation: "Help! We need some consultants!" Case interviewers love these problems.

The best and the brightest

Translation: your interviewer and everyone else who works with him or her at the firm.

Airplane test

Translation: a common postinterview discussion point in the recruiter lounge. Alternatively known as the Pittsburgh airport test. That is, the recruiter is thinking to himself, "Would I be able to stand it if I had to spend an eight-hour layover with this person in the Pittsburgh airport due to a snowstorm?"

Blinding insight

Translation: the unexpected "Aha!" point the recruiter is waiting to see the candidate discover as he or she plows through the details of the case question.

Poet

Translation: a person who breaks out in a rash when he sees anything quantitative. Warning: Never admit to being a poet during the case interview process. Even if the person doing the interviewing was a poet before he joined the firm, he'll have too deep a sense of shame to admit it.

Actionable

Translation: advice or recommendations that the client can really use. Even an exceptionally astute analysis will benefit from a couple of actionable recommendations thrown in at the end. (After all, you want to impress on your interviewer that you really are going after a business job instead of an academic position!)

Sanity check

Translation: one last consideration of your final answer or recommendation. You will be enveloped in detail as you solve a case. Always go back and ask yourself the simple questions of, "Does this make sense?"

80/20

Translation: an efficient approach to solving a case. Careful not to get bogged down in tons of detail, but rather focus on the 20 percent of an analysis that drives 80 percent of the answer. Efficient problem solving!

Case Interview Prep

- Consulting Framework Toolbox

- Consulting Frameworks 101: The First Stage

- Ten Tips for Secretly Impressing Your Interviewer

- Consulting Frameworks 102: A Touch of B-School

- What to Do When You Realize You're in Trouble

- Consulting Frameworks 103: The Whole Shebang!

- Your Own Flavor

- Extra Credit

- Guide to Interview Language

Consulting Framework Toolbox

By this point you understand what the case interview is, you think you have an idea what the consulting firms will be looking for, and you are starting to think that, yes, possibly, you might be able to survive at least the first-round interview. But you're still a little unsure about how to attack these case questions. In particular, you're not clear on how to apply a framework to answer the question. Well, don't worry! WetFeet has prepared a toolbox filled with many of the most famous, and infamous, consulting frameworks around. We call it the Consulting Framework Toolbox, but you can just call it the WetFeet mini-MBA program. (All right, maybe that's a little grandiose, but hey, this report doesn't cost $60,000 either.)

What Is a Framework?

Hold on—you say that you're sick and tired of hearing about frameworks—that you're not even sure what they are? It's actually quite easy. A framework is simply a structure that you use to organize your thoughts and help you analyze the critical issues of a sample case. Think of the framework as your road map through the case. At the simplest, most basic level, your framework can be something as obvious as saying, "There are three key questions that need to be answered here: A, B, and C." At its most complex, your framework can be something as gnarly as the notorious Porter's Five Forces. (If you don't know about Porter's Five Forces: (a) don't worry if you're an undergrad—we'll explain later; (b) worry a lot if you're an MBA.)

Deciding which framework/structure/road map to use may indeed be one of the most difficult parts of the case interview. Once you choose, your path lies

in front of you. But just as you wouldn't use a map of the western United States to navigate your way through New England, you don't want to use an operations framework if the case question is really about marketing. There are as many different frameworks to work with as there are different consulting firms. We provide a thorough overview of framework types in the section that follows.

Choose your framework wisely, and once you choose, tie it to the case example at hand. For example, if you are using costs and revenues as your framework (a simple but rigorous framework and one of our favorites for evaluating a new investment opportunity), you might say something like, "Your question asks whether the company should build a new plant, and I think to approach that question we'd have to evaluate the costs and the benefits. As I see it, the costs for a venture like this will include those from the following three areas . . . while benefits would potentially be realized in the areas of X, Y, and Z. Let's explore each of these areas a little more in depth." The point, then, is not to try to impress your interviewer with the most complex, diamond-studded, and difficult-to-follow framework—you are both likely to get lost in the glitz. Choose a framework with which you are comfortable and which addresses the interviewer's question, identify it upfront, and walk your interviewer through it step by step.

Consulting Frameworks 101: The First Stage

Case Interview

Some of the most flexible, useful, and durable frameworks are also some of the easiest to remember. These include the following: internal/external, costs/revenues, cost/benefit, and supply/demand. The advantage of these basic frameworks is that they are easy to remember and easy to apply to a variety of case problems. The negatives? Well, they're a little simplistic and they may not help you to remember all the points you need to hit in your analysis—particularly in more complex case questions. Nevertheless, the basics are always a good place to start, and these frameworks can often be used in combination with other approaches.

Internal/External

Application: The Firm vs. the Market/The Firm vs. the Competitive Environment Questions

The internal/external framework is a good starting point for case questions that ask you to look at a firm and its environment or market. For example, if you were asked to explain why a transportation client's capacity utilization was down, you might start off with something like, "I'd want to look at both internal factors affecting the company's performance and the external environment in which it found itself. On the internal side, I'd analyze the company's operations, including its scheduling and routing systems, its sales efforts, and its capacity-management processes. On the external side, I'd want to analyze what

was going on in the marketplace. Perhaps the industry is suffering from chronic overcapacity, or perhaps competitors have adopted a new pricing structure that is affecting demand for the client's services. . . ." In general, try to present a balanced equation—three external factors and three internal factors.

Cost/Benefit

Application: Evaluating New Business Opportunities, Business Strategy Questions

A cost/benefit framework can be used to evaluate many different business questions. In particular, if you are asked to make a strategic recommendation for a hypothetical client, you won't go too far wrong by beginning with a list of the costs and benefits for a given action. This is often a good way to start if you aren't sure right upfront what the best approach would be to answering the question. For example, let's say the case interviewer says that you are working for a brokerage house and they are considering installation of an automated order-processing system. "A brokerage house," you think to yourself, ". . . I don't know anything about the securities industry!" Don't fear—the old, trusty cost/benefit framework will set you on your way. You might start by saying something like, "To assess this opportunity, we'd have to look carefully at the costs and benefits of the proposal and try to quantify them wherever possible. For example, some of the key costs of a new automated order processing system would probably involve the hardware and software development, the marketing to support the new program, and customer service. . . . On the benefit side, we'd want to look not only at the new-client business that could be generated, but also at the incremental business that could be drawn from existing customers. We'd also want to examine the potential to achieve savings in operating costs. . . ." Go, go, go, you consulting-interviewing machine!

Supply/Demand

Application: Market Analysis, Business Strategy, Product-Pricing Questions

The supply/demand framework is the granddaddy of economics frameworks. Keep this baby handy for many of your market-analysis and business-strategy-type questions. It will also work well in combination with a number of other frameworks. It will help you explain how actions that affect price or supply might have an impact on market equilibrium (and vice versa).

Since supply and demand are such basic tenets of microeconomic theory, don't be surprised if your interviewer pulls out a pad of paper and says, "Here's what the supply-and-demand situation in the VCR industry looked like in 1990. Show me how it has changed through the present." If this happens to you, don't look at your interviewer open-jawed and wide-eyed because you've never seen supply and demand curves before. If necessary, pull out your micro text right now and do a quick review.

Try sketching this case question below. Remember, demand curves are downward sloping!

Price

Quantity

(The correct answer shows a big backward shift in demand as DVD players gained prominence in the market and a resulting shift down in supply as the market responded to a decline in price levels.)

Marginal Cost Analysis

Application: Questions Asking about Profits or Operations

Marginal cost analysis is one of those nice specialized mini-frameworks that makes an ideal add-on to a larger, more general framework such as cost/benefit analysis. Since microeconomics is really economics of the firm, there is a good chance that you will be able to apply some of your favorite micro-charts or insights to a particular business problem you get from the interviewer. In particular, a tool such as marginal cost analysis may come in handy when you are asked about profits and operations issues. For example, you might be asked about a situation in which sales have gone up as profits have gone down. Now, there are many possible explanations for such a scenario. However, one possibility is that the increased volume has caused the production to exceed the point where it is at its most efficient. In other words, the marginal cost (the cost of producing each additional unit of output) is going up. This could result from the need to purchase raw materials at a premium to get quick delivery. It could result from having to pay workers overtime to fill orders. It could result from any one of a number of things. Although you will probably score extra points by incorporating academic concepts in your answer, keep in mind that the real world is never as clean as the textbooks. You'll undoubtedly want to embellish your answer with messy things like stakeholder interests and organizational dysfunction.

Fixed Cost/Variable Cost

Application: Questions Asking about Profits or Operations and New Business Opportunities

Cost accountants rejoice! Many a case question has been clarified (if not solved) by juggling a few numbers. One thing you'll almost always want to watch out for in profitability-type questions and operations questions is the fixed cost/ variable cost dynamic. Fixed costs are those things such as rent, administrative division salaries, interest on debt, and overhead expenses that can't really be adjusted right away. In contrast, variable costs are those costs, such as those of raw materials, that vary directly with production. These factors can also be important in assessing opportunities in new industries. If there are high fixed costs associated with a new venture, that means that capacity utilization will be key to making the venture work. You might hear a case question along the lines of, "The largest paper manufacturer has announced plans to build a new plant. Should our client, the number three paper manufacturer, follow step?" When you do, think about incorporating a discussion of fixed and variable costs into your response.

The Good Old 2 x 2 (That's Two by Two)

Application: To a Consultant, Everything in Life Can Be Explained with a 2 x 2

Take it from us—your consulting friends can explain everything they see in terms of a 2 x 2 matrix. A good matrix can communicate a difficult-to-under-stand concept in a clear and compelling manner. However, even if it doesn't communicate a particularly exciting message, a good matrix always has the power to wow an unsuspecting client—and consultants just love to do that.

One of the most famous consulting matrices is BCG's Cash Cow 2 x 2, which is used as an analytical tool in product portfolio analysis. It is designed to position a group of products into one of four distinct quadrants:

	Market Share High · · · · · · Low	
Market Growth High	Star	Problem Child
Low	Cash Cow	Dog

The beauty of this matrix is its simplicity. By selecting two measures of product performance (market share and market growth rate) that can run in parallel or in opposite directions, suddenly we have a visual tool for evaluating all sorts of things, like the attractiveness of going into a new market or acquiring a target company. CEOs aim to establish product portfolios chock full of Stars (high market share and high growth) and Cash Cows (high market share, low growth) while divesting themselves of the low-share, low-growth Dogs. Now, no matrix is perfect, and the BCG matrix has been criticized by some theorists as leading in certain circumstances to the wrong conclusions (e.g., some high-growth markets are not attractive for certain businesses). Nevertheless, as a quick-and-dirty tool to analyze market opportunities and product portfolios, it serves its role with flying colors.

WetFeet®

The 2 x 2 matrix is especially useful when analyzing a marketplace, assessing competitors, evaluating product portfolios, or trying to sort out a complex pile of data. And the good news is that not every matrix needs to be as sophisticated as the BCG matrix . . . even if you're interviewing with BCG!

Try Your Hand at 2 x 2s. Now that you know how a 2 x 2 can be used, give it a try! For example, let's say you are looking at a new product-introduction case. Should we launch a new cereal, and if we do, will it eat up our existing brand? "Well," you might say, "Let's look at the industry as it stands today. We have sweetened and unsweetened cereals, and we have cereals that get soggy in milk and those that stay crispy. If we draw a 2 x 2 of the marketplace, we have a whole bunch of brands occupying this upper right-hand Cap'n Crunch quadrant that represent sweetened, stay-crisp cereals. . . ." Hey! You're on your way.

The WetFeet Interview Coach

Draw a matrix representing the breakfast-cereal market.

Ten Tips for Secretly Impressing Your Interviewer

1. Draw a graph for anything. Make sure you draw it horizontally, as all bona fide consulting slides require a 90-degree shift in the orientation of the paper. If you use quadrille paper, your interviewer will really be impressed!

2. Imply, but don't say directly, that you did most of the heavy lifting in your study groups.

3. Use the term "capacity utilization" somewhere in your analysis.

4. Imply, but never say, that you really are impressed by the perks you'll get as a consultant.

5. Talk about how you love intellectual challenges.

6. Ask your interviewer to tell you about the people at his or her firm.

7. Throw in a couple of 2 x 2s or other graphical representations of the data you are presenting.

8. Ask (with a hint of excitement in your voice) how many cities your interviewer has been to in the last year.

9. Ask your interviewer what he or she hopes to learn from work over the next year.

10. Come up with several reasons why you really do think the interviewer's firm is better than the others. Do your company research!

Consulting Frameworks 102:
A Touch of B-School

Slightly more sophisticated than the simple frameworks is a grab bag full of favorite business-school tricks. In contrast to the simple tools mentioned so far, these frameworks and tools may provide a more comprehensive and robust structure for addressing a specific case question. It's important that you know these frameworks—they'll demonstrate to your recruiter your aptitude for approaching business-strategy questions. However, be careful in how you use them—if you're just trying to get fancy without a solid understanding of the underlying concepts, we advise you to stick to the basics.

The 3Cs

Application: Business Strategy and New Market Opportunity Questions

The famous 3Cs stand for customer, company, and competition. These will often be three of the most critical factors to consider when you look at a strategic, marketing, or performance question. Thus, if you're asked to figure out how an auto maker should assess its opportunities in a foreign market, you might start by analyzing what kinds of customers it will find in the new market. You'd probably want to analyze both the individual characteristics of the customers as well as the marketplace's characteristics and trends. A look at the competition would include both an analysis of the competitors in the new market as well as the competitors in the client's existing markets and how all competitors would respond to your client's expansion plans. Finally, the company

analysis would likely include a look at the client's strengths and weaknesses, its internal resources, its longer-term strategy, and how well situated it is to handle the different issues you identified in the customer and competition pieces of your answer.

The 4Ps

Application: Marketing and New Product Development Questions

Here's a favorite one from the Marketing Hall of Fame. The 4Ps are product, price, promotion, and place (distribution). The idea here is that these 4Ps are the four major knobs you can turn when trying to market a new or existing product. Product incorporates everything about the design of the product; its features; how it is different from competing products and substitute goods; its packaging; reputation, service, and warranties; and what the strategy for the product is in the future. Price deals with both retail price and discounts, as well as economic incentives to the different channels (commissions and margins) and the strategic elements of the pricing decision. Promotion has to do with everything from marketing and advertising to customer education, public relations, and franchise or reputation development. The fourth P, place, is really a "D" in disguise. It stands for distribution, and covers such things as choice of channels, cost and duration of distribution, and positioning strategy. An example of a case question for which a 4Ps framework would come in handy is, "Our client plans to introduce a new gourmet low-fat frozen dessert. What are some of the issues we should examine?"

What to Do When You Realize You're in Trouble

Despite your best efforts to avoid getting in trouble during your consulting interview, you will occasionally find yourself far along a dead-end road. The quickest way out of this situation would be to stand up and leave the room. But before you shoot yourself in the head, you just may be able to recover some of your lost ground by taking a few simple steps. We asked our consulting industry insiders for suggestions about what to do when a candidate suddenly realizes she has become mired in the La Brea Tar Pits of consulting-interview oblivion. Here are some of their tips:

1. When you get a question about which you are really uncertain, try to find an answer (or at least get partial credit) through the process of elimination. For example, you might say something like, "Possible approaches to a problem like this would be to look at X, Y, and Z. However, for the following reasons, I don't think those lines of inquiry will produce the ultimate solution."

2. When you run out of ideas halfway through your answer, pause, take a breath, and say, "I'd like to take a minute to think this through." It's okay to not say anything for a minute or two. Collect your thoughts, and write down a few notes if necessary before starting back into the case.

3. If you feel your wheels starting to spin, say, "As I'm working through this, I know I'm starting to get into too much detail. I think the major issue for the client on this front is X. In addition, I know that we still need to talk

Case Interview

about costs and revenues, and I'd like to discuss those areas before time runs out."

4. Tell the interviewer that you believe you misinterpreted the information and explain why you now think your response has missed the mark. Say that you think another approach would be a more productive path to the solution. State what that approach would be.

5. Say, "I'm sorry. Is this a consulting interview? I must have gotten here by mistake. I'm actually supposed to be meeting with Goldman right now."

Consulting Frameworks 103:
The Whole Shebang!

The final category of consulting frameworks incorporates several of the concepts presented above. These powerful, but complex, frameworks are very useful in providing a comprehensive analysis of a specific industry or opportunity.

Porter's Five Forces

Application: Firm Strategy and New Business Opportunity Questions

Although eager-beaver MBAs may be a little bit too anxious to bring Michael Porter into every case question that comes their way, Porter's Five Forces theory is probably the best-known and most powerful industry analysis framework. It can be applied to virtually any industry—from disposable diapers to educational software to automobiles to chocolate. This framework is particularly useful when you want to answer a case question that asks about firm strategy, especially with regard to opportunities to enter a new field. In case you can't already recite Porter's Five Forces in your sleep, here's a little review.

May Porter's Five Forces Be with You

The five forces that purportedly define the nature of a given industry are as follows:

1. **Barriers to Entry** (the ease with which new firms can enter the industry)

2. **Bargaining Power of Buyers** (the relative power of customers and other buyers)

3. **Bargaining Power of Suppliers** (the relative value of vendors and other suppliers)

4. **The Availability of Substitute Products** (the "uniqueness" of the firm's products)

5. **The Nature of the Rivalry Among Firms** (the rationality of competition in the industry)

Analysis of each of these categories and their relevant subcategories should give you a good idea about whether the opportunity looks positive or negative. It will also potentially fill up the entire interview hour, which is not necessarily a good thing for your career interests. We have included a more detailed example of how this framework might be applied to a specific case below. However, the key insights that this analysis will often provide include the idea that an industry is more attractive if there are significant barriers to entry, neither buyers nor suppliers have great power over the players in the industry, there are few adequate substitute products, and the firms are not engaged in an insane competitive rivalry that depresses profits.

Firm Analysis

Application: Business Strategy Questions

Although it doesn't have the brand-name appeal of the Five Forces, Firm Analysis is a robust consulting framework that will often prove helpful in answering case questions. The foundation of the Firm Analysis framework is the identification of the internal (company) and external (market) factors which both come together to influence a company's competitive strategy.

Internal factors influencing a corporate strategy include the following:

1. Company strengths (or, if you prefer, core competencies) and weaknesses

2. Company objectives, values, and mission

3. Company systems and resources

External factors influencing a corporate strategy include the following:

1. Industry trends

2. Outside constraints (governmental, societal, legal)

3. Competitor activities

The business strategies that will likely prove most successful for the firm are those that find a close fit between the internal (company) and external (market) factors. This framework can be applied to many types of strategy questions, especially those involving a new opportunity, a new market, or changing circumstances in the industry. For example, if you're looking at the opportunity for a medical device manufacturer to set up a new production facility in France, you might start by looking at internal factors related to the company's strategic objectives and resources and then move on to the various external factors it will face as it explores the market opportunities in Europe.

Financial Analysis Framework

Application: Product-Profitability Questions

Do your eyes glaze over when the cocktail party discussion turns to costs of goods sold and accounts receivable? Join the club. You'll be glad to know that financial statement analysis doesn't usually warrant the "framework" label.

However, a very basic understanding of how balance sheets, income statements, and cash flow statements work and what messages they can communicate can be a quite important part of your consulting case interview. WetFeet strongly recommends a quick review; our crash course begins below. Financial statements, like frameworks, are roadmaps. If you can navigate the income statement, balance sheet, and cash flow statement, you'll be able to cut through the fluff and identify the core issues of many case questions. In particular, financial statement analysis will be helpful if you find yourself facing a question about product profitability. For example, if you were asked why a steel company was unable to offer a competitive price for its galvanized products, you could structure an answer around an analysis of the various components of product cost:

Basics of the Income Statement

Gross Revenues (= units X price)

subtract	Returns and Allowances
equals	**Net Sales**
subtract	**Cost of Goods Sold**, comprising the following four items:
	Direct Labor
	Direct Materials Costs
	Overhead (watch out for allocation!)
	Delivery Costs
equals	**Gross Margin**
subtract	Selling, General, and Administrative Expenses
subtract	Depreciation
equals	**Operating Profit**
subtract	Interest Expense
equals	**Profit Before Taxes**

direct materials, direct labor, and overhead. You would probably also want to take your analysis a step further by looking at how overhead was being allocated or how sales were being handled.

Basics of the Balance Sheet

ASSETS

Current Assets

Cash	A
Short-term investments	B
Accounts receivable	C
Inventories	D
Prepayments	E
Total Current Assets	**A + B + C + D + E = F**
Property, plant and equipment	G
Less allowance for depreciation	H
Investments	I
Other Assets	J
Total Assets	**F + G + H + I + J**

LIABILITIES AND STOCKHOLDERS' EQUITY

Current Liabilities:	
Accounts payable	K
Loans payable	L
Income taxes payable	M
Dividends payable	N
Total current liabilities	$K + L + M + N = O$
Long-term debt	P
Deferred income taxes and noncurrent liabilities	Q
Total Liabilities	$O + P + Q + = R$
Shareholder equity	S
Common stock	T
Retained earnings	U
Total Stockholders' Equity	$S + T + U = V$
Total Liabilities and Stockholders' Equity	$R + V$

Case Interview

Basics of the Cash Flow Statement

CASH FLOWS AND OPERATING ACTIVITIES

Net income	A
Adjustments to reconcile net income to net cash from operating activities:	
Depreciation expense	B
Amortization of intangibles	C
Gain on sale of plant assets	(D)
Increase in accounts receivables (net)	(E)
Decrease in inventory	F
Decrease in accounts payable	(G)
Total $B + C + (D) + (E) + F + (G) = H$	
Net cash provided by operating activities $A + H = I$	
Cash flows from investing activities	
Sale of plant assets	J
Purchase of equipment	(K)
Purchase of land	(L)
Net cash provided by investing activities $J + (K) + (L) = M$	
Cash flows from financing activities	
Payment of cash dividend	(N)
Issuance of common stock	O
Redemption of bonds	(P)
Net cash provided by financing activities $(N) + O + (P) = Q$	
Net increase (or decrease) in cash $I + M + Q = R$	
Cash at beginning or year S	
Cash at end of year $R + S$	

Your Own Flavor

Tired of all those boring B-school frameworks? Well, you can always create one of your own. One consultant to whom we spoke successfully created a list of key issues that were likely to come up in various types of case interviews (competition questions, new-product questions, business-unit strategy questions, etc.) and used it to sail through the interviews with flying colors. Be warned, however! If you choose to fly solo, you may get high points for creativity, and you'll certainly stand out from other candidates, but you'll also run the risk of missing key issues. WetFeet recommends that you road test all new frameworks before you whip one out of your bag of tricks during your interview.

Extra Credit

A typical consulting case, and most consulting case interviews, will have a few tricky twists and turns—sharp corners where most people go shooting off the highway, or, at best, onto a side road that most people wouldn't even notice. You don't need to nail these to pass the case, but a "blinding insight" may give you a few extra credit points and help you stand out from the crowd. Identifying and analyzing most of these unusual situations will require you to draw on your own resources and insight. However, to level the playing field just a little bit between the former consultants and those who are new to the field, we have included references to a few of the favorite twists and turns. You might want to keep these in the back of your mind, just in case you get through the case and want to pick up a couple of extra-credit points. Remember, though, that the key to a successful case interview is to answer the core portion of the case question correctly.

Damn those unions! Unions, noncompete agreements, government regulations, and parent/sister company relationships may present unexpected constraints to a traditional company that wants to enter a new industry. For example, if a newspaper company wanted to compete in the fast-moving online services area, it would potentially face a severe cost disadvantage because most of its workers are unionized.

Capacity constraints. Costs may jump significantly if new capacity can only be added in large chunks. For example, an auto company might be able to increase production up to full capacity, but, if it wanted to increase production after that, it might have to build a new facility, thus raising per-unit cost significantly if all the capacity weren't completely used.

Economies of scale? Not necessarily! Just because a company has larger volume production it doesn't necessarily have a lower cost structure. Think about the airline business. Profitable regional carriers have often had trouble expanding their business to a national market. Although some systems costs go down as scale increases, other costs may actually rise. Workers may unionize and negotiate higher wages, equipment costs may go up, advertising costs may increase, and the costs of establishing new facilities in different cities may be quite high.

Competitor actions don't always make sense. The dynamic of competitor interactions may make nonsense out of your precise industry analysis. For example, in a declining industry, firm rivalry may be intense, causing firms to drive profits out of what might otherwise be a lucrative industry. Also, long-standing feuds between different players may cause them to act in ways that have no economic justification.

Culture clash. Strong-culture organizations and weak-culture organizations have very different attributes—and neither is necessarily a sustainable competitive advantage. Organizational culture may have a significant impact on how effectively a firm can pursue a new strategy. Think about a strong-culture company such as IBM. For years Big Blue defined itself as a mainframe computer company. As a result, when the market began to shift in the 1980s from mainframes to PCs, IBM went through a period of denial, continuing to invest hundreds of millions of dollars in big computers that the market wasn't buying. This left the door wide open to a band of wily new competitors in the PC industry, such as Compaq, Dell, and Apple. Interestingly, another strong-culture company in the computer industry, Hewlett-Packard, was relatively successful in identifying new market opportunities and continuously reinventing itself to pursue such opportunities (in fact, it entered the PC market itself in 1995 and quickly rose to the top ranks of the industry). Ironically, after merging with Compaq in 2002, HP has been faced with the difficult challenge of combining two strong cultures

Case Interview

(not to mention building shareholder value in the face of a commoditizing industry where Dell is winning).

Is there an accountant in the house? Cost allocation problems can truly distort management's perceptions of product-line profitability. Let's say your client has two products: one is in production 80 percent of the time and is highly profitable; the other only runs 20 percent of the time and is only marginally profitable. If you require each product to carry half the overhead costs, you may announce that it doesn't make sense to produce the second product, even though you can sell it at a price above its variable cost. Wrong!

Guide to Interview Language

In addition to knowing the buzzwords you'll hear during the interview, you should also be prepared to toss a few buzzwords of your own in the direction of your interviewer. To help you draw that ever-so-important picture of you-as-consultant, WetFeet has included a short vocabulary list for your use. Feel free to add to this list as your creativity allows.

During a Consulting Interview . . .

How to Describe Yourself	How NOT to Describe Yourself
Self-starter	Vacation-oriented
Analytical	Inflexible
Out-of-the-box thinker	Silicon
Goal-oriented	Bodacious
Leader	Unprincipled
Resourceful	Touchy-feely
High-energy	Combative
Inquisitive	Weak-kneed
Hard worker	Indecisive
Team-oriented	Follower
Successful	Status-oriented
Numbers-oriented	Whiny
Eager to learn	Ill-mannered
Positive	Short-tempered
Experienced	Vengeful
Recently married	Previously dinged

WetFeet®

The Recruiter's Perspective

- From the Recruiter's Side of the Table

- The Judge's Scorecard

From the Recruiter's Side of the Table

Wow! You're probably thinking that there's an awful lot to keep straight and an awful lot you'll have to do to impress your consulting interviewer. In one sense you're right; case questions can be quite complex. After all, they're often drawn straight from the consultant's work experience. Clients may have paid millions of dollars for the person sitting in front of you and a bunch of her colleagues to spend months studying the very problem the interviewer expects you to analyze in eight and a half minutes. In another sense, however, almost all cases can be boiled down to a few common themes. Remember, the case is ultimately a way of testing to see whether you might be cut out for a career in consulting. And on that front, all of the firms are looking for a few standard things.

Fortunately, your interviewer generally will not be looking for the one right answer to the problem. There probably isn't one right answer; business problems are rarely that simple. And, even though they do want you to hit on a few key issues, most interviewers will be looking for other things from you. In addition to all of the general points she will have been assessing since the start of the interview (e.g., your composure, your communication skills, your experience, and your energy level), your interviewer's mental scorecard during the case question will look something like the following:

- Do you have a logical, clear, and effective way of tackling a simulated business problem? Can you pick out and use a relevant structure or framework to understand and answer the question?

- Are you analytical? Do you think in boxes, tables, and bullet points? Can you pick out key issues of the problem and move through them in an organized and logical way?

- Are you likely to be happy as a consultant? Do you seem to relish the challenge of the mental wrestling matches required to solve difficult problems? Do you ask probing, insightful questions?

- Do you have good business intuition? Do you understand some of the basic business issues? Most importantly, do you push toward action?

- Do you have a consulting "presence"? Are you calm and poised? Can the interviewer see you standing up in front of a middle-aged client and having enough credibility to leave that client thinking that he has gotten the best analysis that money could buy?

The Judge's Scorecard

To give you a better sense of exactly what that consulting firm interviewer is thinking about as he pushes and prods you through the case question, WetFeet has developed the Judge's Scorecard (aka the Consulting Interview Evaluation Form). Think of the scorecard as the tool your interviewer is using to evaluate you. Just in case you're wondering, this is a generic form developed by WetFeet, based on material used by several different firms. Naturally, each firm will have its own approach.

Recruiter's Perspective

Consulting Interview Evaluation Form

Candidate: _____ Round: _____

Date: _____ Interviewer: _____

School: _____ Case Used: _____

Ratings: Please assign a rating for each category and an overall rating at the bottom.

1 = Excellent/Good   2 = Average/Neutral   3 = Poor/Unsatisfactory

Rating	Skill Category	Comments
	Analytical Skills	
	Comfortable with numbers?	
	Identifies key issues?	
	Identifies appropriate frameworks?	
	Follows a logical approach?	
	Problem-Solving Skills	
	Intellectual curiosity?	
	Breaks problem into parts?	
	Draws on previous experience?	
	Out-of-the-box thinking? Results Orientation	
	Starts with issues that provide leverage?	
	Uses realistic, doable approaches?	
	Focuses on actionable items?	
	Listening Skills	
	Listens carefully to problem?	
	Asks questions when necessary?	

Recruiter's Perspective

🗀 Consulting Interview Evaluation Form (cont'd)

Rating	Skill Category	Comments
	Presentation/Communication Skills	
	Clear and to the point?	
	Credible?	
	Responds well to questions/challenges?	
	Uses analogies and examples effectively?	
	Personal Attributes	
	Intelligence	
	Maturity	
	Integrity	
	Common sense	
	Team player	
	High energy	
	Fit with Culture	

Office/practice preference: _____

Overall candidate rating: _____

(1 = Recommend against passing to next round; 2 = Neutral; 3 = Recommend for next round)

Interviewer's signature: _____

Case Examples

- Good Cases for Good Consultants-to-Be

- Suggested Answers to Case Questions

Good Cases for Good Consultants-to-Be

At long last, here they are! Real, live sample case questions and suggested answers. To help you prepare for the case interview, we have first listed the questions for which we will provide sample answers. If you wish to simulate the case interview process, you might start by jotting down your own notes about the question before you look at the sample answer. If that sounds about as exciting as doing division longhand just for the sake of keeping your arithmetic skills sharp, then go ahead and look at the answers. They begin immediately after the questions.

Case Question 1

List several ideas for improving the customer service level of an airline's ticketing call center.

Case Question 2

A U.K. banking client asks, "Should we acquire a stock brokerage firm on the Continent?"

Case Question 3

The manager of the on-campus coffee shop comes to you for advice. Last quarter a food service workers' strike shut down the campus cafeteria for nearly three weeks. He thought this would be great news for the business—the coffee shop was packed. Now that the numbers are in, however, he finds that even though the coffee shop had record revenues, it made a loss for the quarter. What happened?

Case Question 4

How many golf balls would be used in the United States in a given year?

Case Question 5

You are assisting a regional Bell operating company (RBOC) that has been attempting to diversify its business lines outside of the traditional telephone business. Unfortunately, it has been unsuccessful in a number of previous new ventures, including real estate, financial services, and software. This time, the client is considering an opportunity to get into electronic home security. The attractive features of this industry include:

- Relates well to phone company's core business (phone lines, operator services, installation services)

- No big players in the industry (five largest firms have combined total of less than four percent market share)

- Large potential demand (only ten percent of residences have security systems)

- Long-term customer value is high (equipment is low-margin business, supervision services high-margin)

Question: Is this a good opportunity? What do we need to know to assess the opportunity?

Case Question 6

A leading manufacturer of instant cameras and one-hour photo finishing machines is facing a dramatic downturn in business due to the rapid increase in digital photography and sharing photos over the Internet. What should it do?

Case Question 7

Rather than go into consulting, you've decided that you want to start a natural-flavor frozen-sherbet business. You've done some research and discovered that Häagen-Dazs has the following value chain. Draw a similar value chain for your start-up business and explain how and why it would be different.

Value Chain Comparison: Ice Cream

Häagen-Dazs   **Start-Up**

$1.00

$0.22 margin

$0.09 overhead

$0.10 shelf space

$0.20 advertising

$0.05 cold storage
$0.03 distribution

$0.08 processing

$0.05 packaging

$0.15 cost of goods

$0.00 $0.03 R&D

The WetFeet Case Analysis Worksheet

Use this form to sketch out your answers for the sample cases provided in this WetFeet Insider Guide.

Type of Question: _____

Frameworks that Might Prove Useful:

_____

_____

_____

Questions to Ask/Additional Information Required:

_____

_____

_____

Most Important Issues:

_____

_____

_____

The WetFeet Case Analysis Worksheet (cont'd)

Outline of My Answer:

_____

_____

_____

_____

Action/Implementation Implications:

_____

_____

_____

_____

Twists and Turns:

_____

_____

_____

_____

Suggested Answers to Case Questions

The following are suggested answers to several different types of questions. To give you more insight into what would be expected of you, we have included key tips and notes in addition to the suggested answers.

Case Question 1

Question

List several ideas for improving the customer service level of an airline's ticketing call center.

Background

Consultants will often ask you to *list* several potential solutions to a particular problem in rapid fire sequence *upfront*. In an interview, this approach may be experienced as a discrete "case" question or as part of a larger, more structured and complex case. It will sometimes be used to assess out-of-the-box thinking quickly when interview time is short. This question type aims to assess your creative ability to generate several possible solutions or hypotheses from the start in order to guide a deeper, structured analysis later on. This is a very effective approach in consulting, because it drives creative brainstorming upfront— before getting enveloped in extreme levels of detail—generating a hypothesis-driven start to a client case.

In general, no list is right or wrong. The interviewer is most interested in seeing you propose some clever, original thoughts about a problem, even if they seem far-fetched. Therefore, the key to a successful answer here is to have fun with the challenge. Since your interviewer will be looking for a combination of creativity and analytics, don't hold back! If this were a team meeting and you were trying to identify solutions to a client problem, the goal would be to get as many ideas as possible out on the table and to select the most important ideas for further analysis. This question could be given to undergrads, MBAs, or advanced-degree candidates.

Suggested Response

There is no single right answer to this question—especially given that the interviewer wants you to provide a laundry list of ideas—but there are lots of good answers. Even when the interviewer wants a quick list of thoughts, it is not a bad idea to put a quick structure around it. For example, you might point out that you can improve customer service in two overall ways, by perception and by reality.

To improve perception, you may suggest adding music to the wait time to make it seem shorter. Also, the initial recorded message could have a "hook" to keep people listening longer (i.e., rather than just pushing "0" immediately), such as an announcement like, "please listen to the entire message, as our menu has changed." The airline could also offer exciting promotions that customers are interested in hearing more about before moving on to the customer service person. Some creative thinking could also be applied to the automated message itself, like making the recorded voice more friendly or allowing the customer to select options by speaking, as opposed to by dialing.

Next would be examples of the second type of service improvement, actually improving response times, information accuracy, and overall efficiency. If

adding customer service representatives is not an option due to costs, the airline could ensure that the reps are well trained on using their systems so they are able to navigate information and transactions quickly. Periodic surveys could also be conducted with customers to identify and prioritize key areas of needed improvement. Phone systems could be configured so that if a rep needs to forward a customer to another rep, there is a personal handoff with all three people on the line, as opposed to simply forwarding a customer to another automated response and wait cue. The airline may also be strategic in setting their customer cues by prioritizing customers who are frequent fliers or those who are calling to actually purchase a ticket. Further, the airline could keep a log of each customer so that the rep immediately knows his or her preferences for seating, flight times, and so on. Finally, the airline could incentivize its reps by the number of happy customers, as identified through random surveys.

Case Question 2

A U.K. banking client asks, "Should we acquire a stock brokerage firm on the Continent?"

Suggested Response

In this sample response, we provide a dialogue with notes on what's being said (in italics). Remember, however, there really isn't any one right answer for a case question. This response is meant only to suggest the types of issues you might want to talk about with your interviewer. That said, aren't you psyched that we're walking you through a real, live case . . . and that you didn't get stuck with this question in your case interview! This question would probably be given to MBA candidates.

Interviewer: You're working for a bank in England. The chairman comes to you and says, "I think we ought to acquire a brokerage firm on the Continent, but I'd like your opinion on that." What should you say?

Beware of the overly general question! The interviewer will often start off with something so broad and general that it is impossible to answer. The interviewer is really trying to see if you will take the bait, or if you will keep your wits about you and ask for more information.

Candidate: Well, I'd probably start by asking, "What do you mean? Are you thinking about acquiring a specific firm? Are you interested in entering a specific country or market? Are you thinking about getting into the stock brokerage business in general?" Alternately, I might ask the chairman about the fundamental objectives he is trying to accomplish. Is he seeking an entree into the brokerage business? Is he trying to boost revenues? Does he want to expand in Europe?

It is usually okay to ask for more information, especially if you have just received the case question. Often, the interviewer's response will give you a hint as to what angle to pursue. However, don't just ask questions for the sake of taking up time. They should be designed to give you enough information to proceed with the case.

Interviewer: The chairman says that he wants to explore opportunities generally and that he doesn't have a particular firm or target country in mind. He is interested in increasing the bank's base of operations on the Continent and the brokerage industry seems to have a lot of smaller, profitable players that may be ripe for acquisition.

The interviewer is directing the candidate towards a general strategy response. Therefore, the key issues will center on the firm (its strategic objectives, its strengths and) and the opportunity (macroeconomic issues as well as the identification and evaluation of specific acquisition candidates).

Candidate: It sounds like a general strategy/acquisition study might be in order. Since the client doesn't have any specific markets or acquisition targets

in mind, I'd want to start by analyzing both internal and external issues for the client.

By starting with a general statement, you can check in with your interviewer to see if you are on the right track. If you have missed the boat, some interviewers will gently push you in another direction (but beware, others may let you drown!).

Interviewer: Why don't you start by telling me some of the key internal issues you'd look at?

The interviewer likes the candidate's top-level internal/external framework, but is a little wary of the use of acquisition study. She wants to make sure the candidate really understands what information he needs to identify.

Candidate: On the internal side, I'd want to look at four or five key things: the client's strategic objectives for the acquisition, its core strengths and weaknesses, its existing business operations and systems and how those might fit with a potential acquisition, and the resources it has available for the acquisition.

The candidate has set up a sub-framework to focus his response about the internal issues the client will face. Although these points don't follow any standard framework, they do include a mix of strategic and operational issues.

Candidate: Of these issues, I'd start with a look at the client's strategic objectives for the acquisition. Frankly, the first question I would ask is whether or not the client ought to be acquiring a new business in a different market. Is this part of a broader diversification or internationalization strategy? Is the client just trying to use up some excess cash?

A key challenge in many real-life consulting cases is to accurately define the right question to ask. In this response, the candidate questions the initial assumption that an acquisition is called for. An alternative approach would be to assume that the decision to acquire has been made and the consultant has been called in to implement. In this case, the candidate would probably want to state the assumption and move on to analyze the various internal factors he has outlined.

Candidate: After determining its strategic objectives, I'd like to analyze any strengths and weaknesses that would be relevant to the acquisition. Does the client have a particular set of resources that make an acquisition of one type or another fit better with its existing organization? Perhaps it already has banking affiliates in several other European countries. Perhaps it has relationships with a number of banking customers that are active in certain areas on the continent. Are there particular service or product offerings that it is seeking to add to its portfolio? By looking at these issues, I would be attempting to establish some parameters by which to evaluate different investment options. In particular, I would be looking for areas in which the client may be able to achieve synergies or significant cost savings.

The candidate works his way through his framework, focusing first on the issues that will yield the greatest insight. He also offers some examples, in the form of questions, that indicate the types of issues he will be looking for. Finally, he mentions how he will use this analysis to produce a recommendation for the client.

Interviewer: What other things would you need to know to give the client your recommendation?

Here the interviewer poses a question that could be approached in different ways. The candidate could continue to explore internal issues, or he could move over to some of the more important external issues.

Candidate: There are still several issues on the internal side that I haven't yet explored, such as the internal systems issues and the budget for the acquisition and so on. However, for the purposes of making a recommendation to the client, some of the external issues are even more important, and I'd like to talk about some of those now.

> ### Insider Tip
>
> It is a good idea to briefly point out instances in which you stray from your initial framework. That way the interviewer won't assume that you just lost your way.

Here the candidate interprets the question fairly literally and moves on to issues of primary importance to making a recommendation to the client.

Candidate: On the external side, I'd want to break this into three basic pieces. The first involves taking a macro look at the marketplace for brokerage services across Europe. For the second piece I would identify potential acquisition candidates and assess their attractiveness based on the parameters we had identified. After a broad-based look at a number of candidates, the third piece would involve a detailed evaluation of three or four of the most promising firms.

Although the candidate hasn't called on a Porter Five Forces/3Cs gourmet flavor of consulting framework, he has identified a logical approach to getting at the answer. In addition, he has helped his presentation by saying that there will be three pieces to the analysis and clearly stating what those pieces will be.

Interviewer: Let's use your approach and start with a look at the market for brokerage services in Europe. What would you look at?

Candidate: Well, Europe consists of a lot of different countries and, I expect, a lot of different rules and regulations on brokerage services. I think the best

way to start would be to analyze the various markets we were thinking about entering and determine which would offer the most opportunity for an investment by a British bank.

To do this, I would want to look at two sets of factors for each country. [*Geez, can you believe how good this guy is?*] First, I'd start with a survey of the overall market situation. How big is the country's GDP, what is the structure of its economy, how fast is it growing? I'd also want to analyze its stock market. Some countries may not even have stock markets, others may have really small capitalization. There may be regulations about foreign ownership.

Simultaneously, I'd want to look at the brokerage business in each market. How is the stock market set up? How many firms compete in the brokerage business? Who owns them? How profitable are they? What are the key resources that give one an advantage over others?

Again, the candidate gives a structure to his response. "First . . . Second . . ." This helps the listener follow the presentation. Also, he identifies a number of areas of potential concern: underlying economics, regulatory issues, and competitive rivalry.

Interviewer: How would you go about getting that information?

Consultants are data hounds. A key concern in many interviewers' minds (especially for undergraduate candidates) is how resourceful the candidate will be in gathering information.

Candidate: Well, I'd probably start by seeing if there were any internal resources that might contain some of that information. It's possible that somebody within the organization might have researched the same topic for another study or might be familiar with certain aspects of brokerage markets in Europe. Beyond that, I'd probably identify resources within each market

that provided the kind of information we needed. These might include the equivalent to the SEC or the authorities in charge of the various stock markets. They might include other banks or competitors in the industry, or they might include printed resources or databases. At some point, when it came time to evaluate the various acquisition candidates on the shortlist, I'd think we'd need to utilize some secondary means of evaluating their performance, such as utilizing customer surveys or speaking with experts in the field.

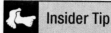

Insider Tip

If there are particular pieces of analysis with which you feel more comfortable than others, you can often jump directly to those by saying something along the lines of what this candidate just said.

The candidate starts by looking as close to home as possible. He also seems to be aware of many of the favorite resources for consulting studies. Importantly, he hasn't suggested any ideas that would be completely unfeasible, such as interviewing the heads of the SEC equivalents in each country.

Interviewer: Okay. You've gone out, collected a pile of information about three or four different potential candidates. How would you finally choose among them?

The interviewer is testing to see whether the candidate will be able to do something with all of the analysis he has offered.

Candidate: Well, I'd want to go back to the initial parameters I developed after looking at the internal factors. In particular, I'd want to see which acquisition opportunity seemed to offer the best fit with the client's long-term business strategy and organization. In particular, I'd want to see evidence that the acquisition would bring some source of competitive strength to the client,

whether it be in terms of market access, or in terms of a set of synergies between the acquisition target and the client that would allow the client to operate the company more efficiently. I think I'd also want to assess the various types of risk with the proposed acquisition.

The candidate goes back to the start of his analysis and incorporates the internal factors identified and analyzed early in the case problem as the relevant considerations in developing a recommendation. In addition, he focuses on several issues that are critical to any successful acquisition.

Interviewer: Oh? What types of risk would you look at?

The interviewer chooses to examine one small piece of the candidate's answer and see if he really has thought this through carefully. The interviewer is also testing to see if the candidate can identify a key issue about deregulation. The interviewer is also being incredibly anal. Give this guy a break! Pass him on to the next round!

Candidate: Well, a key risk in Europe would be to think about the impact of European deregulation. Any profits that we had anticipated earning as a result of the acquisition would have to be considered in light of future stock market deregulation. In addition, we'd also want to look at other risk categories such as management risk, technology risk, and other market risks.

The candidate does a good job of listing several risks and offers the information the interviewer is seeking about the effects of deregulation.

Interviewer: Good. Well, it looks like we've covered most of the issues I wanted to go through with this case. Now let me ask you about another situation.

Candidate: Ahhhhh . . .

General Summary Comments

This was clearly a question about business strategy. In his answer to the question, the candidate identified a few simple frameworks and structures that helped him touch on a number of issues associated with the problem. He also did a relatively good job of letting the interviewer know where he was and what was coming next.

Case Question 3

The manager of the on-campus coffee shop comes to you for advice. Last quarter a food service workers' strike shut down the campus cafeteria for nearly three weeks. He thought this would be great news for the business—the coffee shop was packed. Now that the numbers are in, however, he finds that even though the coffee shop had record revenues, it made a loss for the quarter. What happened?

Background

This a business operations problem of the declining-profits variety. In this one, the interviewer is looking for your business intuition and for your ability to apply this intuition in chasing down the answer to the problem. This question would be appropriate for undergrads as well as MBAs and advanced-degree candidates.

Suggested Response

Candidate: There are a variety of things that could cause revenues to go up while profits went down. I'm not sure which is the most likely—maybe the manager was skimming some money off the top? Just kidding! The first thing I'd like to know is whether there were any other unusual expenses during the quarter. Did costs go up? Was there a write-off of some sort? Was the coffee shop dealing with expenses carried over from a previous period? Did it have to

hire on additional labor at a premium or pay overtime to serve all those additional customers?

It's often a good idea to make sure that you have the whole picture. Case interviewers will often leave out critical details to get you to start off in the wrong direction. In addition, they may be trying to see if you will actually step back and take a critical look at the situation before you dive in. In a case such as this one, where there could be a number of possible explanations, it's good to see if you can get some more hints from your interviewer. At the same time, the candidate has already provided some structure to her answer by focusing on the cost/expense side first.

Interviewer: I'm a little bit curious as to why you would immediately assume there was something illegal going on. However, in answer to your question, no. There weren't any extraordinary expenses in the quarter. No lawsuits for bad food, no acquisitions of new equipment. What else could have happened?

Candidate: Hmm. Well, if there weren't any unusual expenses, I'd want to look at the other pieces of the costs and revenue equation. On the revenue side, we assume that sales volume went up significantly as a result of the cafeteria closure. Since total equals price times quantity, I wonder if the prices the coffee shop charged for its products went down. Did it change its pricing structure?

Since her first approach didn't yield any results, the candidate is taking a step back and becoming a little more systematic in her approach. Although she might have been better off labeling it as such, she seems to be backing into a framework based on the "profits = revenues − costs" equation. One good thing is her mention of the revenue equation.

Interviewer: No, the prices remained the same.

Candidate: Then we need to continue looking at the other pieces of the cost and revenue equation. You said there weren't any extra-ordinary expenses, but what about changes in the normal expenses of the operation? Did raw material prices go up? Did rent, utilities, or trash-removal costs go up as a result of increased volume? How about spoilage?

The candidate still hasn't figured out exactly why the profits went down, but she is doing a good job of systematically exploring various reasons why this might have occurred. Also, she is doing a good job of explaining how she is thinking through the problem. Thus, the interviewer knows that she isn't just bopping around from scattered thought to scattered thought.

Interviewer: No, these all remained relatively stable on a per-unit basis.

Candidate: Something clearly changed from the previous quarter. Since we have ruled out changes in prices and significant changes in expenses, then there was something else going on. We know that sales went up. We also know that customer flow went up and that people who usually eat at the cafeteria were coming to the coffee shop. Therefore, it's possible that this new customer group was different from traditional customers. One strong possibility is that they were ordering different items from traditional customers. Specifically, since they were using the coffee shop as a substitute for their usual cafeteria dining, it's possible that they were ordering more food than the traditional customer.

The candidate has systematically worked her way toward a possible explanation. By thinking out loud, she reveals that she didn't immediately know the answer. However, she has demonstrated a relatively logical approach to problem solving and hypothesis testing that will be useful as a consultant.

Interviewer: That's correct. There was a new type of customer with a new purchasing pattern. But what does that tell you about profits?

Candidate: I would assume that many of the new customers came in to get food. Therefore, the product mix sold during the quarter probably changed. Since we know that there weren't any extra-ordinary expenses, and since we know that profits went down, we have to assume that the coffee shop was sucking wind on the food business.

Interviewer: Bingo!

The candidate has come up with the correct answer by systematically going through the example and focusing on the various components of the key equation. In addition, she has demonstrated to the interviewer that she can think logically and use a framework effectively.

General Summary Comments

Many case interviews will ask about a situation in which profits are declining. Although many of these questions may be more complex than this one, it is a good idea to keep the profit and revenue equations foremost in mind as you work your way through them. In this case, a change in product mix was the key. Another typical problem may deal with fixed and variable costs.

Case Question 4

How many new golf balls would be used in the United States in a given year?

Background

No consultant wannabe can expect to cruise through the case gauntlet without skirmishing a time or two with the old market-sizing question. Typically, these questions take the form of "How many telephone poles are there in the United States?" or "How would you go about figuring out the market for interactive TV?" Short, sweet, and relatively easily dispatched, these questions will often serve as a warm-up question for a more lengthy case. Alternatively, they might

be hidden within the context of a larger strategy-type question, during which the interviewer will ask the candidate to discuss how he or she would go about estimating the market size for a particular product. Market-sizing questions like this one could be used for undergrads, MBAs, and advanced-degree candidates.

In any case, when the interviewer throws you a market-sizing question, she is trying to check you out on a couple of things. First, she's trying to see if you have an allergic reaction to numbers. It's not necessary that you be the next math-jock superstar, but, if you can't think through a few simple BOE (that's "back of the envelope") addition/subtraction/division types of operations, or at least recognize the need for them, you may face some tough sailing in the consulting world. Even more importantly, the interviewer wants to see if you can identify what you need to know, make a set of realistic assumptions, and come up with a solution.

Suggested Response

You might start by saying that the basic drivers (no pun intended!) in the golf ball market are the number of golfers in the United States, the number of balls they use per round, and the number of rounds they play per year. To figure out what that actually means, you'd need to make some assumptions. Assuming there are 300 million people in the United States and that 20 percent of the population plays golf, you'd guess that there are 60 million golfers in the United States. If you figure that golfers play an average of ten rounds per year, and that they use two to three balls per round, you'd come up with a number around 1.5 billion golf balls.

After that rough calculation, you might want to go back and talk about other factors influencing the golf ball market and how they might affect your estimate. Things that might increase the number of balls used in the United States include nongolfer purchases. For example, you might hypothesize that driving ranges and

pro shops could account for significant purchases, thereby increasing the number of golf balls sold. In addition, you might mention that there is probably a small niche market of tourist purchases of golf balls—especially Japanese tourist purchases. Finally, a certain percentage of golf balls never actually sees any use. Most golfers have a few extra balls hanging around inside their bags or garages. All of these factors would increase the market size for golf balls.

In addition, you ought to also discuss factors that would decrease the market size for U.S. golf balls. For example, you could mention that there is a substantial market for used golf balls, which would decrease the numbers of new balls purchased. Also, golfers often find lost balls when they are looking around in the weeds, further decreasing their purchases of new ones.

General Summary Comments

Once again, the goal here really isn't to come up with the right answer. The goal is to come up with a realistic answer based on reasonable assumptions and a methodology that shows you understand some key drivers behind the problem. In this example, you probably want to attach a few more numbers to some of your adjustments to the basic market size you derived. In addition, the interviewer might push you to explain some of your insights further.

Case Question 5

You are assisting a regional Bell operating company (RBOC) that has been attempting to diversify its business lines outside of the traditional telephone business. Unfortunately, it has been unsuccessful in a number of previous new ventures, including real estate, financial services, and software. This time, the client is considering an opportunity to get into electronic home security. The attractive features of this industry include:

- Relates well to phone company's core business (phone lines, operator services, installation services)

- No big players in the industry (largest five firms have combined total of less than four percent market share)

- Large potential demand (only ten percent of residences have security systems)

- Long-term customer value is high (equipment is low-margin business, supervision services high-margin)

The Question: Is this a good opportunity? What do we need to know to assess the opportunity?

Background

Hey! It's an industry strategy question of the new-opportunity variety. The interviewer here has given the candidate more complex information about a particular case and wants the candidate to go through an analysis of the opportunity. Since this involves a new business opportunity, there will be relevant issues both on the company side and on the market or opportunity side. The key is to choose a good framework and start sorting through the issues. MBAs would probably be the most likely to receive this question. However, undergrad and advanced-degree candidates might receive a pared-down version.

Suggested Response

Identify a few top-level issues and ask which to pursue. The interviewer's question has a good bit of detail in it, but to decide which angle to pursue, you probably want to ask a few general questions first. Therefore, you might start by pointing out a few of the key areas you see as most relevant to responding to the question. First reaction: There are a couple of top-level questions that jump out from this case. First, is the electronic security business really a good business to get into? What are the underlying economics? Second, is this a

good business for the client to pursue? Does it fit with company strategy? Does the client bring anything to the business? Third, given the company's failure at other ventures, there is a larger question about whether or not the client is organizationally set up to handle any kind of new business venture, let alone this one.

At this point, the interviewer will likely offer some indication about which angle to pursue. Lacking a suggestion, pick the angle that you think will be the most productive to pursue, both for the value it will yield for the client and for your level of insight into the issue. In this case, you might start with an assessment of the industry.

Choose a framework: How about supply/demand? If you want to explore the industry, there are several logical frameworks that would provide a useful structure for the answer. One easy approach would be to look at demand and supply in the industry. Only ten percent of the population have alarm systems, but this may be a mature market. Is demand stable? Are unit sales and customers growing? Are prices going up? At what rate? What is happening over the longer term? Is the market saturated? Who are the customers, what makes up demand? How have fears of terrorism altered the landscape? How do customers make purchase decisions? What about the supply side? What drives supply? How many firms are competing? What type of firms are competing? How are they competing? What are the margins in this industry? Is there an opportunity to come in with a differentiated product? Is there an opportunity to decrease the cost structure through economies of scale? What would be the reaction to entry by the client?

Or maybe the 3Cs? Another slightly more complex approach would be to look at the famous 3Cs: Customer, Company, and Competition. Here you'd want to think about what kinds of people are actually buying home security

systems and how that would affect the opportunity for the RBOC. You'd also analyze the skills and weaknesses of the client as they relate to the electronic security business. Finally, you'd need to look at the competition. Who are the other players? Why are they or aren't they successful? Is there any consolidation going on?

Let's try the Five Forces. Finally, you might be tempted to whip out the BMW of consulting case frameworks, the Porter Five Forces industry-analysis framework, to analyze this opportunity. As you know from your recent strategic management course and this WetFeet Insider Guide, the five forces include: supplier power, buyer power, threat of potential entrants (barriers to entry), and the availability of substitute products. All of these feed into the final force, rivalry among firms in the industry.

Porter One: Fragmentation may indicate intense rivalry. You might want to comment first about the fact that the industry is highly fragmented and therefore seems likely to feature intense rivalry among the competitors. Why is it that there aren't any big players? Are there advantages to being small? One logical possibility is that localized, personal service is very important to customers—not a promising environment for the likes of the phone company. Another possibility is that there really aren't many economies of scale to be gained by a larger operation. In particular, it's not clear that the monitoring (high-margin) portion of the business benefits by centralization and cost reduction. These factors don't eliminate this as an opportunity for the client, but they do suggest that additional questions ought to be asked.

Porter Two: Check to see whether consolidation really makes sense in this industry. On the other hand, we know that there are sometimes great returns to be made from consolidating a fragmented industry. To see whether these opportunities exist, we would need to look at general trends that are tak-

ing place today. Is consolidation already occurring? Clearly, the client has the financial power to compete strongly with smaller operations. However, in the security business, big may not necessarily be better. Local players will always be coming in and trying to compete, and many of them may have noneconomic motivations for entering and staying in the business. The phone company, which will be focused on the bottom line, may have difficulty competing against such players. Finally, the demand in the industry isn't clear. Is this market saturated, or are there significant opportunities to create new demand?

Porter Three: Barriers to entry seem to be low. After looking at the rivalry issues, you'd also want to talk about the barriers to entry. If the client went into the business, there wouldn't be a whole lot of things keeping other competitors out. The business probably isn't regulated. The technology doesn't seem to be proprietary. There aren't necessarily large capital requirements to get into the business. It is possible that branding the service would create wider customer recognition and provide protection against potential competitors. However, the product really doesn't seem to be very differentiated right now. Therefore, this raises a question about how defensible a position the client would be able to create for itself. This would tend to argue against making an investment here.

Porter Four: Buyer power. For the most part, it seems that buyer power in the industry is relatively weak. Most customers make one-time purchase decisions at one location. This weakens their power vis-à-vis suppliers. Customers aren't going to be able to provide the service themselves, so if they want to buy electronic security, they will need to acquire it from a provider. And after they have a service up and running, most people are probably disinclined to change carriers. However, the buyers aren't without any power. They have lots of suppliers to choose from, and their switching costs are probably quite low.

Porter Five: Supplier power. The supply side of the equation doesn't seem to pose any great problems here. Security providers basically buy security equipment and monitoring devices and hire staff to watch them. Although there may be some significant players on the supply side (we'd want to check out whether or not this is true), it doesn't seem like the client would be in a weak negotiating position there. There could potentially be some threat of forward integration by security-device providers. However, if anything, given the phone company's resources and experience with technology and data transmission, it would likely be the most integrated player in the field. It would also probably have the greatest market power given the large resource base it has.

Change Gears: How to create a good business here? At this point (or perhaps before this, if your interviewer is getting bored with the Porter shtick), you will likely be asked to explain one set of issues in detail. For example, you might be asked to explore the issues of sustainable competitive advantage in greater detail. "How would the client potentially go about creating a thriving business in electronic security?" To explore this issue, you probably wouldn't immediately have a handy-dandy framework nearby. However, you might start by saying that you like to analyze three or four different sources of potential competitive advantage and what they would mean for the client.

First-mover advantage. First, if the industry really is as fragmented as has been described, the client would have a potential first-mover advantage in establishing a brand name and differentiated service product. By getting out there first and offering a reputable and recognizable product, the client would be able to generate word-of-mouth sales and set the service standards to suit its own competitive strengths. This would be a source of potentially sustainable advantage for the client in the short run. However, to develop this business would require a substantial initial investment and ongoing expenditures to

maintain its position. Over the long run, this is not a definitive source of advantage that would allow significantly higher rents.

Low-cost supplier. Second, given its existing capabilities, the client has the potential to occupy a low-cost supply position. However, this is by no means certain. You'd have to start by analyzing the economics of the business. Are there equipment supply and installation costs that would drop as volumes increased? Possibly, but, remember, installation is the low-margin portion of the business. Would the monitoring portion of the business allow substantial cost savings as scale increases? It's not at all clear that it would. The key is probably capacity utilization. How is an operation like this manned? You need to make sure that you can handle all calls at peak periods. However, you also don't want to have fixed salary or other costs that are being carried by a very small number of customers.

That brings up another point. How productive is the phone company staff? It's certainly not known for being the world's most efficient. And given the difficulty of dealing with union contracts, it may be at a cost disadvantage. How about customer acquisition? It's possible that the client could achieve important cost savings here. Since it has a large network of phone service customers, it has ready access to names and addresses of potential customers. In addition, it could potentially reach them more cheaply than could the competition. On the other hand, the typical industry player today sounds like a local operation. Therefore, it might be hard for the phone company to compete with the local security company whose president goes to the same church and plays golf at the same courses as do his clients. On balance, then, low-cost position offers at best a mixed message about sustainable advantage.

Branding and reputation. Third, the reputation and name recognition of the client offer greater potential advantages. For a big-ticket purchase like home

security, the customer may be inclined to go with a name brand. In addition, ease of access is also important. It is probably a significant advantage for the phone company to sell these services. Everybody knows how to contact the phone company. Not everybody knows or trusts "Sammy the Security Specialist." At another level, the phone company does have access to the latest technology and expertise in handling that technology. Therefore, it may be able to offer a differentiated product more quickly and easily than many of the smaller, more localized competitors. Also, the phone company's reputation and reach are not things that most competitors will ever be able to match. As a result, this seems to offer the greatest possibility of developing a source of sustainable advantage.

Implementation issues. With all of these points, there is a basic question about implementation. Since a strategy is only as good as its implementation, you would need to consider what approach would best fit with the client's own organization. What is a phone company good at doing? What are its particular strengths and weaknesses? What resources does it have that potential competitors don't? What liabilities does it have?

Let's look at strengths and weaknesses. At this point, the interviewer might turn to you and ask you to go into more depth about the company's strengths and weaknesses. What kinds of things would you need to look at as you develop a strategy? In response, you might do a brief run-through of what you imagine the various strengths and weaknesses of the client to be. In particular, you might mention anything that would offer a particular advantage or difficulty to your client in accomplishing their strategy.

Labor issues. One example that could work either way is the use of phone company labor. Although the phone company has a potential advantage in its

large cadre of maintenance and service people, this may also be a problem on the cost side. In particular, most workers are probably on union contracts and therefore would likely be very expensive. In contrast, most of the small competitors would undoubtedly be nonunion.

How to deal with labor issues. The interviewer might then ask you what kinds of strategies would allow you to overcome this difficulty. In response, you might mention several possibilities, such as acquiring a number of smaller local firms, setting up a separate organization outside the phone company superstructure, or even something more creative, such as developing a joint worker-owned and -managed entity with fewer work rules and a different salary structure. The disadvantage of something like this is that it might take a long time to set up. Another alternative would be to use a more highly auto-mated process. However, you'd have to explore the capabilities of the technology to determine the opportunities here.

What else? After the above analysis, you would have touched on many of the issues that the interviewer was hoping to hit. However, there are other things that might have been discussed. For example, you might have talked about how marketing challenges for a business like home security would be very different from those required for the traditional phone business. This would present a potential hurdle to your client. However, by tying up with another firm that specialized in breakthrough marketing the client might be able to overcome its weakness.

Another issue you might have talked about concerns the ultimate size of the business opportunity. Compared with the phone company's core business, the electronic security business will always be small potatoes. There is a question about whether or not it is even big enough to be of interest. If it could be done profitably, it probably is. However, the client would probably want to set

up a separate operating unit or structure that wouldn't be overwhelmed by the comparison with the core phone business.

Finally, you might have chosen to explore some of the issues about the client's previous failed investments. There may be some core issues around its ability to identify and successfully pursue new business opportunities that are much more important to the future of its organization than a small home security business ever would be.

Case Question 6

A leading manufacturer of instant cameras and one-hour photo finishing machines is facing a dramatic downturn in business due to the rapid increase in digital photography and sharing photos over the Internet. What should it do?

Background

This question calls for the candidate to help determine strategic direction in the face of environmental change. As a result, it will be important to look both at what's going on in the marketplace as well as what the company is set up to do. An effective answer to this question will offer a strategy that fits well with the company's resources and objectives. This question could appear in interviews of undergrads, MBAs, or advanced-degree candidates. It would probably be most common in MBA interviews.

Suggested Response

There are several ways to go about looking at the problem. You could use any of the following frameworks: supply and demand, industry analysis, decision trees, internal and external analysis, even the 3Cs. However, for this sample answer, let's say you want to use your own approach. After hearing the question, you might ask your interviewer if you can take just a minute or two to jot

down some thoughts about the problem. On a piece of scratch paper you might write something like:

Market Issues

- Supply shrinks dramatically
- New equilibrium will be lower price, lower quantity
- Competitor response
- Possible substitute markets

Strategic Alternatives

- Find new markets for products
- Find new products to be made with existing assets
- Fight it out for existing markets
- Acquire capabilities linked to digital photography
- Exit from the business

Company Issues

- How will the change in market affect the client?
- Depends on position in the industry
- Product mix (decline in demand unlikely to be uniform)
- Competitive position (is client in low-cost position? High-quality position? How will it fare relative to others?)
- Customer mix
- Pricing, margins, costs

Company Strategy Issues

- What are the other businesses of the client?
- How reliant is it on its traditional photography business?

- What are its strengths and resources?

- How flexible are facilities/labor?

- What is best for the shareholder?

After writing down these notes, you might start right into your analysis. A good first step would be to say that you plan to talk about four different pieces: the economics of the marketplace, the strategic alternatives the client faces, two sets of company issues, and the resources of the client and its strategic objectives. In this way, even though you aren't using one of the famous frameworks, you have mentioned a structure for your answer and identified a mix of relevant types of analysis that you will conduct on your way to making a recommendation to the client.

Once you have identified the different areas, it's a good idea to proceed by saying something like, "I'd like to lay the groundwork by looking first at the economics of the marketplace. We know that the rapid growth of digital photography and the Internet as a sharing vehicle means a dramatic drop in the appeal of instant cameras and the need for one-hour photo finishing. In macroeconomic terms, this will result in a shift downward in the demand curve. (Draw your basic supply and demand graph and show visually what you mean!) As we can see, that will result in a short-term drop in both the quantity and the price levels for the market. Depending on how the different competitors in the industry respond, we will likely see a corresponding shift backward in the supply curve over the medium- or long-term. In practice, that means that the market will likely lose some of its less profitable producers of instant cameras and photo finishing equipment. . . ."

At this point, the interviewer would very likely jump in and ask you how you would estimate future demand in the industry. This could be a little tricky, since the industry faces changes that it has never encountered before. Depending on

the particular segment of the market with which your client deals, you could also probably define and quantify the key drivers of demand. For example, it would be useful to assess whether the convenience of digital photography has raised overall demand for photography. Also, you would want to hypothesize how people will leverage the Internet for sharing pictures in the future—perhaps the joy of viewing a physical print of a digitally generated picture will prevail over viewing via a PC screen. It will also be critical to clearly understand what kind of consumer likes to buy an instant camera, what kind of picture-taking occasion they use it for and whether there may be a niche area of demand going forward. In a market with changing circumstances such as this one, you would want to be sure that you also performed some sensitivity analysis for your numbers. That is, you'd want to make sure that you looked at both optimistic and pessimistic scenarios for market growth.

After going through the most important economics issues, you could move to the second part of your analysis. "Faced with this scenario, the client really has a limited set of strategic alternatives. First, it can remain in the instant camera business and just fight it out with competitors, hoping to maintain a profitable piece of a smaller market. Alternatively, it can attempt to focus on niche areas of demand, such as passport and ID photos, movie set usage for ensuring consistency between takes, humorous photo souvenirs at carnivals, etc. It could also explore less developed foreign markets where digital technology is unaffordable, but the idea of cheaper instant cameras may be of strong appeal. As for its one-hour photo finishing machine business, the client may want to focus on becoming the lowest-cost provider, allowing them to achieve a dominant position as others are forced to exit.

"Second, the client can attempt to use its resources for other purposes. It may have facilities that can easily be shifted into production of digital cameras or related critical components. For example, it might have advanced capabilities in

camera lenses that can be used in digital cameras and sold to digital camera makers that are less advanced in their lens-making capabilities. Additionally, the client might be able to leverage proprietary technologies and expertise in photo finishing to develop high-quality personal printers that consumers can use to print digital pictures at home. It may also make sense for the client to consider strategic acquisitions that could help augment its foray into digital photography (e.g., a digital camera manufacturer or an Internet business specializing in online digital photo sharing).

"Third, the client can decide that it doesn't want to weather the impending battles over a declining market and, as a result, decide to exit the business completely. In particular, if other organizations have not yet decided to sell off any operations, the client may find that it can still get a fairly high return on the sale of its assets linked to traditional picture taking and photo developing…"

After laying out the strategic alternatives, the interviewer would want to see that you had a strategy for deciding among them. Based on the information given so far, you would almost certainly need to ask for more information about things such as the following:

- What comprises the client's overall business, and how much of it is accounted for by instant cameras vs. photo finishing machines?

- What is its position in the industry? Is it in a good cost position? Is it a marginal producer?

- What are its assets like? Can they easily be shifted into production of digital photography products?

- Does it have an adequate sales and service structure to go after niche or underdeveloped foreign markets where digital photography is less pervasive?

- Of the types of products it produces, are there related applications in non-shrinking markets?

- How about the softer issues? What is its vision? What are its company values? What is its culture?

Remember, questions should be linked to your analysis. Don't just ask for the sake of using up air time. It's best if you explain what you are trying to do, what kind of information you need to do it, and how the piece of data that you are seeking will help you answer that question.

As you go through your response, you will likely face a number of questions from your interviewer. Why are you looking for that information? How would you go about finding that information? What kinds of commercial applications might there be for X? What challenges would you face as you tried to move from traditional photography technologies to digital? What are the key differences between the markets? What other unexpected factors might have an impact on this business?

General Summary Comments

There are a number of variations on the digital photography question that might come up in the interviewing room. What happens when a new foreign competitor comes into the industry? How do you respond to a big and sudden change in consumer tastes? The key to answering these questions is to look both at what is happening in the marketplace and how the client is prepared to respond. Again, you don't have to come up with the best strategic game plan for the company. After all, you only have about 15 minutes to examine a complex set of issues. However, the interviewer will be looking for you to approach the problem in a way that will lead you to a good answer. In addition, he will also be looking to see how creative you can be as you think about responding to a changing marketplace. This is a little bit different from questions that ask you to tell an imaginary client how to do a better job of what they're already doing.

Case Question 7

Rather than go into consulting, you've decided that you want to start a natural-flavor frozen-sherbet business. You've done some research and discovered that Häagen-Dazs has the following value chain. Draw a similar value chain for your start-up business and explain how and why it would be different.

Value Chain Comparison: Ice Cream

Häagen-Dazs	Start-Up
	$0.10 margin
$0.22 margin	$0.03 overhead
	$0.10 commisions
$0.09 overhead	$0.10 shelf space
$0.10 shelf space	$0.05 advertising
	$0.05 cold storage
	$0.04 distribution
$0.20 advertising	$0.10 processing
$0.05 cold storage	$0.10 packaging
$0.03 distribution	
$0.08 processing	$0.23 cost of goods
$0.05 packaging	
$0.15 cost of goods	
$0.03 R&D	$0.10 R&D

$1.00 ... $0.00

Background

Case interviewers love to throw in a question or two that call for the candidate to respond to graphs. In one sense, this is an easy way to screen out some candidates. All consultants develop an intimate relationship with their favorite graphs. As a result, the candidate who freezes before the graph like a rabbit in the headlights will quickly become roadkill. If you have a strong aversion to graphs, you might want to think about another profession. If you don't have such an aversion, but you are a little bit rusty, we suggest that you at least pull out that old economics textbook and do a few problems just to build up your strength. You'll probably be glad you did! Although graphs are fair game for all candidates, this particular question would most likely be found in an MBA interview.

Suggested Response

For this response, you'd probably want to work on the graph provided by the interviewer. The question comes with its own framework—you just have to follow along the categories on the value chain. First we'll present one possible answer, and then we'll identify several issues you might choose to mention in your discussion.

R&D

Overall, R&D would be a higher percentage of sales for the start-up.

Reasons the Start-Up Costs Would Be Higher

- New product development from scratch is expensive and is front-loaded
- Development required on a larger percentage of total product line
- Hire on a contract basis rather than permanent
- This is likely to be a key differentiating factor for product (initial success probably not based on traditional marketing or shelf space presence)

Reasons the Start-Up Costs Would Be Lower

- Longer-term product strategy for the start-up probably doesn't require constant new product development—not trying to compete with entire Häagen-Dazs product line

- Shelf-space issue suggests that there is a limited return to product development—since only ten containers fit on a shelf, new flavors will replace existing flavors, not competitor flavors

Cost of Goods Sold

This would be much higher for the start-up.

Reasons the Start-Up Costs Would Be Higher

- Lower volume purchases means that there would likely be higher per-volume costs

- Strategy may be to offer better-tasting products, requiring specialized ingredients, higher quality, higher costs

Packaging

This would be higher for the start-up.

Reasons the Start-Up Costs Would Be Higher

- Lower-volume runs, higher cost per unit, especially because line change-over costs would be significant

- Have to hire outside packaging firm to print packaging

- Shipping and other fixed costs would account for a higher portion of the price

Processing

Costs would typically be higher for the start-up, but in some scenarios could be equal or slightly lower.

Reasons the Start-Up Costs Would Be Higher

- Must hire outside processor to manufacture product

- Timing issues—have to wait for available capacity, scheduling conflicts

- Fewer direct controls over production means possible wastage, more outside supervision costs

- Can't necessarily locate processing plant next to packaging/shipping locations

Reasons the Start-Up Costs Would Be Lower

- Assuming Häagen-Dazs has its own processing plants, it needs to operate at capacity to carry overhead effectively. If it doesn't, and if this is a small-margin operation, cost per unit could be higher if Häagen-Dazs has to carry fixed costs with small volume

- Häagen-Dazs doesn't have any opportunity to negotiate a good price for manufacturing once it has dedicated capacity

- Start-up has some negotiating leverage with processor (Can refuse to buy output if quality is low)

Distribution

These costs generally will be higher for the start-up.

Reasons the Start-Up Costs Would Be Higher

- No high-volume discounts

- No dedicated shipping options

- No distribution facility

- Small-volume deliveries mean much higher labor cost per unit delivered

- Fewer retail outlets spread more thinly

- Velocity of product off the shelves may mean irregular deliveries, which could increase the costs

- No opportunity for delivery people to sell the retailers additional products or collect shelf/competitor information for the start-up

Reasons the Start-Up Costs Would Be Lower

- Serve local geographic region only (short-term advantage)
- Pay only for capacity used

Cold Storage

This would be higher for the start-up.

Reasons the Start-Up Costs Would Be Higher

- No dedicated facilities
- Limited availability of cold-storage locations means that aggressive, large-volume competitors can lock out smaller competitors by tying up all available resources
- Lower volume equals higher prices
- Minimum scale for production may still be higher than current demand, requiring longer cold-storage time before shipment of product

Advertising

This would be lower for the start-up in most cases.

Reasons the Start-Up Costs Would Be Higher

- Lower-volume purchases means higher per-item charge

Reasons the Start-Up Costs Would Be Lower

- Can't afford/don't do end-customer marketing
- Use guerrilla marketing techniques
- Focus on channel sales rather than customer sales
- Not competing with other big ice cream makers

Shelf Space

These costs could be equal, or even lower, for the start-up.

Reasons the Start-Up Costs Would Be Higher

- Big brands with fast-moving volume may get price breaks on shelf space

- Big brands can manage stocking tasks, thereby taking costs out of system or retailer

Reasons the Start-Up Costs Would Be Lower

- Strategy involves selling through retail locations that don't charge for shelf space

Sales Commissions

These would be higher for the start-up.

Reasons the Start-Up Costs Would Be Higher

- Pay brokers on a commission basis for regional sales

- Häagen-Dazs doesn't use brokers, it has a dedicated sales force

Overhead

This would be lower for the start up.

Reasons the Start-Up Costs Would Be Lower

- Work out of apartment

- Get by with much less infrastructure

- No public reporting requirements

- No administrative divisions

Margin

This would be lower for the start-up.

Reasons the Start-Up Costs Would Be Lower

- Made up for by higher retail price

General Summary Comments

There are a lot of different ways in which you could explore this question. Some will be obvious, such as the different costs for purchases for small- and large-volume producers. Others will be less clear, such as the product-development strategy and the shelf-space issues. In addition to seeing whether or not you understand the cost structure of producing a given product, the interviewer will also be testing you to see if you have any business intuition about how to deal with these two very different business models.

For Your Reference

- Recommended Reading

- Additional WetFeet Consulting Resources

Recommended Reading

For Your Reference

Competitive Strategy: Techniques for Analyzing Industries and Competitors

Michael Porter (The Free Press, 1980)

In case you missed it in your business school strategy course, you may want to give Mike Porter a glance. Don't sweat all the details—the practicing consultant who could quote Porter is a real anomaly. Instead, focus on the main points of industry analysis. Porter's first couple of chapters do a fairly good job of introducing his way of picking apart an industry. If you're particularly enamored of one area or another, you can always read further. As much as anything, the Porter book will give you a sense of some of the types of analysis and thinking that consultants are required to do on the job. If you like this stuff, consulting may be a good fit.

Modern Competitive Analysis

Sharon Oster (Oxford University Press, 1990)

Here's another standard B-school strategy text. It's very well written and sprinkled with terms, situations, and frameworks you're likely to encounter in the case interview. In particular, Oster focuses on three areas that will be relevant to many of the business-strategy or operations case questions you might encounter: analysis of the economic environment, analysis of things going on inside the firm itself, and rivalry among firms.

"The Core Competence of the Corporation"

C.K. Prahalad and Gary Hamel (Harvard Business Review, May–June 1990)

Here's a great article that even real live practicing managers have reportedly found useful. New Age business gurus C.K. Prahalad and Gary Hamel discuss

how corporations that effectively identify and use their core competencies are able to maintain their competitive advantage. Just exactly what is a core competency in the Prahalad and Hamel sense? Core competency is the real skill, knowledge, and/or expertise that a company has developed, from which it is able to launch new products and new services, and create new business more quickly than the competition. It is not a specific plant, contract, or resource that diminishes through use. Thus, they identify Honda's core competence in building engines and power trains, Sony's competence in miniaturization, and 3M's competence in sticky tape. For the purposes of the case interview, you might want to analyze the core competencies of a corporation that is thinking about going after a new business opportunity.

Additional WetFeet Consulting Resources

- WetFeet's bestseller *Ace Your Case II: Fifteen More Consulting Cases*, *Ace Your Case III: Practice Makes Perfect*, and our brand new *Ace Your Case IV: The Latest and Greatest* are the perfect complements to *Ace Your Case*, with 15 full-length case questions and answers. For additional practice, get the *Wharton Case Interview Study Guides Volumes I* and *II*, all available from www.wetfeet.com.

- WetFeet.com offers a number of online case interviewing resources at www.wetfeet.com/research/industries/consulting/case.asp.

- For help on creating your resume, check out WetFeet's guide *Killer Consulting Resumes*, available from www.wetfeet.com.

- WetFeet also offers a number of Insider Guides on top consulting firms. These are also available from www.wetfeet.com.